my dear young
friends

my dear young friends

Pope John Paul II

Speaks to Teens on Life,

Love, and Courage

John Vitek, Editor

Saint Mary's Press®

✸ Genuine recycled paper with 10% post-consumer waste.

The publishing team included Steven Roe, development editor; Gabrielle Koenig, production and copy editor; Amy Schlumpf Manion, typesetter; Cären Yang, designer; cover photos by AP/Wide World Photos; manufactured by the production services department of Saint Mary's Press.

The acknowledgments continue on page 121.

Library of Congress Cataloging-in-Publication Data

John Paul II, Pope, 1920–
    My dear young friends : Pope John Paul II speaks to teens on life, love, and courage / edited by John Vitek.
        p. cm.
ISBN 978-0-88489-724-8 (alk. paper)
    1. Catholic youth—Prayer-books and devotions—English. [1. Prayer books and devotions. 2. Catholic Church—Prayer books and devotions.] I. Title: Pope John Paul Two. II. Title: Pope John Paul the Second. III. Vitek, John. IV. Title.
    BX2198.J64 2001
242'.63—dc21

                                                                        2001000979

Printed in the United States of America

ISBN 978-0-88489-724-8

Thank you to the young people across the United States who helped select the quotes for this book, especially Venessa, Amy, Jenn, Emily, Denise, Vanessa, Dana, Josh, Michael, Fred, Matt, and the many others whose names I don't know.

Pope John Paul II first addressed the youth of the world in his apostolic letter *Dilecti Amici,* in 1985. Since then he has addressed youth nearly every year for World Youth Day. Every other year young people from all over the world pilgrimage to a different place of the globe in response to the Holy Father's invitation to attend World Youth Day. This amazing day is a celebration and sharing of faith in Jesus Christ.

The quotes used throughout this book are the actual words of the Holy Father. They have been taken directly from his addresses to young people made during his pastoral visits to various countries around the world. Other quotes come from his prepared remarks, which were meant to prepare young people for annual World Youth Day pilgrimages. Young people from across the United States selected the quotes in this book because they found them to be particularly challenging and inspiring.

Throughout this book you will see citations following each of the pope's quotes, such as "Pope John Paul II, World Youth Day XV." The following list of sources helps explain the citations you will come across in your reading.

Dilecti Amici. Pope John Paul II's apostolic letter on the occasion of the International Youth Year, 31 March 1985

Israel-Palestine. Message of the Holy Father to the young people of Israel and Palestine, 22 September 1999

Poznan, Poland. Address of the Holy Father at the youth meeting in Poznan, Poland, on the occasion of the pastoral visit to Poland, 3 June 1997

Saint Louis, Missouri. Message of the Holy Father to the young people at the Kiel Center, Saint Louis, Missouri, 26 January 1999

Santiago, Spain. Message of the Holy Father to youth meeting in Santiago de Compostela, 8 August 1999

World Youth Day VI. Message of the Holy Father for the 6th World Youth Day, 15 August 1990

World Youth Day VII. Message of the Holy Father for the 7th World Youth Day, 24 November 1991

World Youth Day VIII. Message of the Holy Father for the 8th World Youth Day, 15 August 1992

" I have called you friends, because I
have made known to you everything
that I have heard from my Father."

—John 15:15

Pope John Paul II has a deep affection and love
for young people. Undoubtedly, you—young
people throughout the world—hold a special
place in Pope John Paul II's heart. He has an
extraordinary interest in you. Moreover, he
believes in you—in your hunger for God and in
your desire to do good things in the world.

You, perhaps like no other generation, are
growing up in a world of rapid and constant
change. Yet, in this world of change, you can
find in Pope John Paul II's words an unwavering
constancy. His message is a lasting message of
love and encouragement. He will both affirm
your goodness and challenge you to greater
things.

The Holy Father's desire for you—for all young people around the world—is clear: Draw close to Christ so that you may participate, with the whole community of believers, in the great task of transforming the world according to God's design, of creating a world where the love of God directs all things!

John Paul II believes in you as a young person. He is convinced that in Christ you have the ability to make this world a better place. Through your friendships, your family, your work, your school, and your athletic, artistic, and intellectual talents, you can spread the Good News of God's love in ways that only a young person can.

This is why each time that John Paul II addresses young people he calls out in a special, heartfelt way, "My dear young friends!" His is a friendship with you that is rooted in the Good News of Christ's love. In addressing the youth of Poland in June 1997, John Paul II said: "Dear young people, follow Christ with the enthusiasm of your youthful hearts. He alone can calm [your] fear. Look to Jesus from the depths of your hearts and minds! He is your inseparable friend." This message is just as meaningful to you today as it was to the Polish teens in 1997.

My Dear Young Friends provides you with fifty-two weekly reflections on the Holy Father's words. You will find a quote from the Holy Father for each week of the year. These are the words he would say to you if you were to meet him face-to-face. They are powerful words. They are words that affirm you, challenge you, and call you to a deep and profound love for Christ through his church.

Think About That

Each quote is followed by a section titled "Think About That." When you come to this section, pause to think about what the Holy Father has to say to you. Imagine that he is speaking these words directly to you. What do his words mean to you? What is he teaching you?

Take Action

Following each "Think About That" section, you will find a challenge to "Take Action." These actions are important to carry out. Why? They're important because the Christian life is one of both word and deed. What good does it do to be inspired by the words of our Holy Father but not to integrate them into the way you live your life? The actions do not take a lot of time, but they will help to change your life.

Say a Prayer

The Holy Father also wishes that you pray over matters of faith and life. Each week's reflection provides a prayer. Use this prayer each day of the week to keep the words of the Holy Father fresh in your mind and heart.

Finally, the "Did you know?" section offers you some trivia about the pope's life and ministry. This information will help you come to know the pope in a more practical and personal way.

May the words of our Holy Father inspire you and enliven in your heart a burning fire for the Good News of Jesus Christ!

John M. Vitek
President, Saint Mary's Press

I will not be afraid.

—Hebrews 13:6

" Do not be afraid of Christ! Trust him completely! He alone 'has the words of eternal life.' Christ never lets us down!"

—Pope John Paul II, Poznan, Poland

Think About That

The Holy Father reminds us, "Christ never lets us down!" Never! Sometimes it's hard to believe that, because we all have had the experience of friends who have let us down. But Christ will not. How would our lives be different if we trusted Christ completely? How would we act if we never feared being let down by him?

Take Action

In our friendships, we have surely let others
down. Can you think of a time recently when
you have let down your mother or your father?
Maybe you have let down your friends? Go to
them sometime this week and tell them that
you are sorry for letting them down. Tell them
that you are going to work hard at not letting
them down in the future.

Say a Prayer

Lord, I want to trust you completely. I am so
glad that you will never let me down. If I follow
your ways, I know that I will have eternal life
with you. Thank you.

Did you know? Pope John Paul II was elected pope in 1978 at the age
of fifty-eight. He is the 264th pope in the history of the Roman Catholic
church.

The integrity of the upright guides them.

—Proverbs 11:3

66 But—I ask you—is it better to be
resigned to a life without ideals . . .
or rather, . . . to seek the truth,
goodness, justice, working for a
world that reflects the beauty of
God, even at the cost of facing the
trials it may involve?"

—Pope John Paul II, World Youth Day XII

Think About That

To live in a world where we experience
Christian ideals like kindness, patience, peace,
forgiveness, and joy takes people who first
believe in those ideals and then commit to

acting out those ideals every day. That's no easy task. The Holy Father is asking us, "Is it worth it?" He says, "Yes!"

Take Action

Every day, in many ways, we fail to live out our Christian ideals. Each time we fail, we cause a little "death," or pain and sorrow, in someone and in ourselves. This week, choose one Christian ideal that you are going to work hard to live out in every situation and with every person that you meet.

Say a Prayer

Lord, help me to live out the ideals of Jesus. Help me especially when others make fun of me or tease me for standing up for what I believe in. Help me to know that it's worth the work.

Did you know? The pope has numerous official titles, including bishop of Rome, vicar of Jesus Christ, successor of the prince of the Apostles, supreme pontiff of the universal church, patriarch of the West, primate of Italy, archbishop and metropolitan of the Roman province, sovereign of the state of the Vatican City, servant of the servants of God.

Remember the poor.

—Galatians 2:10

66 Jesus invites us to love the poor,

because they should be given

special attention precisely because

of their vulnerability."

—Pope John Paul II, World Youth Day XIV

Think About That

The poor are vulnerable because they don't
have access to things they need in order to live
a full life. Some don't have access to health
care, enough food, or a place to live. Some

don't have access to a good education or a job. What would your life be like if you didn't have these things?

Take Action

This week, find at least three articles of clothing in your closet or dresser or on your bedroom floor that you don't need. Take them to a place in your town that provides clothing to poor people.

Say a Prayer

Lord, help me to love poor people, and not to look on them as second-class citizens. Help me to give of myself so that they may have what they need to live.

Did you know? In 1958 John Paul II was appointed auxiliary bishop of Krakow, Poland.

I am with you always.

—Matthew 28:20

" *Jesus is living next to you,* in the brothers and sisters with whom you share your daily existence."

—Pope John Paul II, World Youth Day XII

Think About That

Do you mean to tell me that Jesus is living with *those* people next door? No way! But how might I think differently of my neighbors if I accepted that they are my brothers and sisters in Jesus? This is a big challenge that the Holy Father puts to you, because we like to find fault with our neighbors rather than praise them.

Take Action

This week, think of something kind you can do for your next-door neighbor. Then do it!

Say a Prayer

Lord, thank you for living next door to me in my neighbor's home. Help me to see you there. Help me to be kind and good to my neighbors, because you are living there with them.

Did you know? Pope John Paul II was baptized as an infant on 20 June 1920.

They recognized him.

—Luke 24:31

66 Call out to Jesus to remain with you
always along the many roads to
Emmaus of our time. May he be
your strength, your point of refer-
ence, your enduring hope."

—Pope John Paul II, World Youth Day XII

Think About That

Remember the story of the disciples walking
on the road to Emmaus after Jesus' death? The
disciples were despairing. They thought they
had lost their best friend forever. They were

down in the dumps. They were losing hope. Then Jesus appeared and walked with them, and restored their hope.

Take Action

Read the story of the disciples on the road to Emmaus in Luke 24:13–35. This week, pay attention to a friend in school who seems to be in the dumps. What can you do to walk with that friend today, to help him or her have hope again?

Say a Prayer

Jesus, thank you for not leaving us, for always being with us, and for walking by our side. Help me to be a friend like you, to walk with my friends in their time of despair, to bring them a sense of hope in your name.

Did you know? In March 1943, Pope John Paul II had his first lead role in the theatrical performance of *Samuel Zborowski.* It was also his last theatrical performance.

Be hospitable.

—1 Peter 4:9

66 There, in the midst of humankind, is
the dwelling of Christ, who asks you
to dry every tear in his name, and to
remind whoever feels lonely that no
one whose hope is placed in him is
ever alone."

—Pope John Paul II, World Youth Day XII

Think About That

Think about the way that Jesus lived his life. He
visited the sick. He went out of his way to be
with people whom others didn't want to be

around. He helped people up when they were down. He shared in people's sorrow when they were sad. This is what we are called to do too.

Take Action

You know that some kids in your school cafeteria sit alone for lunch each day. They seem not to have any friends, right? At least one day this week, take your lunch tray and sit with someone who usually sits alone. Ask if you can join him or her for lunch. See if you can't get to know him or her a little bit.

Say a Prayer

Lord, you went out of your way to be with people who were alone. Help me to have the same kind of courage.

Did you know? The armored car that the pope uses is actually called the popemobile. It has an electronically controlled seat and a motorized elevator platform for getting in and out of the car.

Seek to do good to one another.

—1 Thessalonians 5:15

" Do not be satisfied with mediocrity. The kingdom of heaven is for those who are determined to enter it."

—Pope John Paul II, Santiago, Spain

26

Think About That

Maybe you've heard the phrase, "If you're going to start a job, then finish it." Well, that's basically what the Holy Father is saying. If you're going to love God, then love God completely. If you're going to be kind to someone, then don't be just a little bit kind. Be completely kind. If you are going to forgive someone, forgive completely, not just partially.

Take Action

This week, say at least one kind thing to every person you meet. This is not easy. It requires determination. At the end of the week, give yourself a score. How did you do?

Say a Prayer

Lord, help me enter the Kingdom of heaven by living my life the way you want me to live it every day.

Did you know? Pope John Paul II was ordained a priest on 1 November 1946.

Love one another.

—1 John 3:23

" May you experience the truth that
he, Christ, looks upon you with
love!"

—Pope John Paul II, *Dilecti Amici*

Think About That

Looks are a powerful thing. The way someone
looks at you sends all kinds of messages to you.
You know the difference between someone
who looks at you with love or care or concern
and someone who looks at you with dislike or
anger or envy. Well, Jesus looks at you with love
every day!

Take Action

This week, be conscious of how you look at other people—at home, at school, at work (if you work), and around your community. What are you thinking about when you look at the people you encounter this week? Each time you look at someone, look at her or him with a sense of care, concern, or joy in your heart. Notice how you look at people differently when you do this than you would otherwise.

Say a Prayer

Lord, let my eyes be your eyes. Let me look on everyone I meet in the same way you look on me—with love.

Did you know? Pope John Paul II refused to have a coronation when he was installed as pope. Instead he was installed during a Mass in Saint Peter's Square.

My peace I give to you.

—John 14:27

" Dear young people, make your generous and responsible contribution to the constant building up of the Church as a family, a place of dialogue and mutual acceptance, a space of peace, mercy and pardon."

—Pope John Paul II, World Youth Day XII

Think About That

The Holy Father believes in you. He believes that young people can make a big difference in the world and in the church. He's asking you to make the church—the community of people who believe in Jesus—a place of peace, mercy, and pardon. Are you up for the challenge?

Take Action

This coming Sunday when you are in church and it is time to give the sign of peace, turn to at least five people that you don't know and offer them the sign of peace.

Say a Prayer

Lord, help me to be a peacemaker, someone who shows mercy toward others and who forgives others when they hurt me.

Did you know? Pope John Paul II has traveled around the world to visit his people more than any pope in history has. He has traveled more than half a million miles since becoming pope.

We are ambassadors for Christ.

—2 Corinthians 5:20

" Christ has made you his ambassadors, the primary evangelizers of your contemporaries."

—Pope John Paul II, World Youth Day VIII

Think About That

An ambassador is someone who represents something to others. For example, we have ambassadors from one country to another. The ambassadors represent their country, and the other country expects the ambassador to act for and make decisions for their home country. So too we are to be ambassadors of Jesus Christ. We are to represent Jesus to others, especially our peers.

Take Action

This week, start a Bible study with some of your friends. You don't need to have an organized meeting. Just ask some of your friends, some people at school, or people in your youth group if they would like to meet this week to read from the Bible and talk about what it means. Your parish priest or youth minister probably has lots of resources to help you.

Say a Prayer

Lord, thank you for inviting me to be an ambassador for you. Give me the strength to represent you faithfully.

Did you know? A complete description of Pope John Paul II's papacy can be found on the World Wide Web at *www.vatican.va/holy_father/ john_paul_ii/index.htm.*

Clothe yourselves with love.

—Colossians 3:14

" God is love; every person is loved by God, who expects to be welcomed and loved by each one."

—Pope John Paul II, World Youth Day XII

Think About That

God expects us to welcome and love him! Why? Because God is love and God loves us! Love is God's gift to us. It is because of God's love that we are capable of loving others and of being loved by others.

Take Action

What is one thing you can do this week to show that you love God? Maybe you can help out around the house in a special way. Maybe you can talk to someone at school who doesn't have a lot of friends. Maybe you can tell your mom or dad that you love them, and thank them for their love.

Say a Prayer

Dear God, help me to love you. Thank you for loving me first so that I can love others.

Did you know? As a young man, Pope John Paul II enjoyed athletics, philosophy, poetry, and drama.

Do not seek your own advantage.

—1 Corinthians 10:24

66 The human being has a deep-rooted tendency to 'think only of self.' . . . One who chooses to follow Christ, on the other hand, avoids being wrapped up in himself and does not evaluate things according to self interest."

—Pope John Paul II, World Youth Day XVI

Think About That

The Holy Father tells us that those who follow Christ see life as a gift, and those who follow only their own desires see life as something to be conquered and possessed. The pull to follow our self-interest is strong, but ultimately empty and false. Christ's way of self-giving is the path to true life and joy.

Take Action

On one side of a sheet of paper write the word "self-centered," and on the other side write the word "Christ-centered." This week, before going to bed each night, reflect on your day. Under "self-centered" write all the ways you focused only on yourself, your needs and desires. Under "Christ-centered" write all the ways you gave of yourself to others.

Say a Prayer

Dear Lord, forgive me for the ways in which I focused only on myself today. Help me to think of the needs of others and to respond to their needs in the way you would want me to.

Did you know? As a young man, Pope John Paul II loved to perform. His first theatrical performances were in the years 1934–1938, while he was in secondary school.

You shall be happy.

—Psalm 128:2

" Wherever I go I challenge young people—as a friend—to live in the light and truth of Jesus Christ."

—Pope John Paul II, Saint Louis, Missouri

Think About That

You hear and see many things every day that try to convince you they will bring you real happiness—like the right clothes, the right friends, alcohol, and so on. But the truth is that living in the light of Jesus Christ is the only thing that brings real happiness and joy. Only when we live the way Jesus wants us to live can we be happy. The Holy Father, as our friend, tells us this is true without a doubt.

Take Action

Can you think of one thing that people say will make you happy? Is it something that is consistent with what Jesus teaches? If not, ask yourself, "Will this really make me happy?" Now what do you want to choose? Do you want to follow false truths, or do you want to follow Jesus Christ who is the truth and the light of happiness? Your action step this week is to choose which path you will take.

Say a Prayer

Lord, help me to choose your truth today and always.

Did you know? Pope John Paul II was born on 18 May 1920.

Christ has set us free.

—Galatians 5:1

" Now Christ says: 'You will know the truth, and the truth will make you free' (John 8:32)."

—Pope John Paul II, *Dilecti Amici*

Think About That

How can the truth make us free? Well, think about it. When you tell a lie, what do you feel inside? You feel really yucky and kind of tied up in knots, right? Lies tie us up—we're not free. But truth does the opposite. It unties us. It makes us feel good inside. It sets us free because we don't have the fear of being caught in a lie.

Take Action

This week, find a short piece of rope about 3 or 4 inches long. Tie the rope in a knot and stick it in your pocket. Carry that piece of rope with you all week. When you get in a situation where you feel the need to tell a lie—even an itty-bitty lie—reach in your pocket and feel that knot. Ask yourself, "Is this how I want to feel inside?" Untie the knot. Tell the truth, and feel what being free is like.

Say a Prayer

Lord, you are the way, the truth, and the life. Help me always to choose to be free by telling the truth.

Did you know? Sometimes the pope is affectionately referred to as Papa. This comes from the Greek word *pappa,* which means "father."

I am poor and needy.

—Psalm 40:17

66 Dear young people, I invite you especially to take concrete initiatives of solidarity and sharing alongside and with those who are the poorest. Participate generously in one or another of the projects through which, in different countries, others of your contemporaries are involved in gestures of fraternity and solidarity."

—Pope John Paul II, World Youth Day XIV

Think About That

The Holy Father is inviting us to move way outside our comfort zone. He's asking us to travel to the parts of the world where the poorest of the poor live. He invites us to get to know poor people as our brothers and sisters.

Take Action

This week, call your parish youth minister or the diocesan office and ask if they know of organized programs for mission trips to other parts of the world. Study, reflect on, and pray about what you learn. Listen to God in prayer to hear how you are called to participate in this mission.

Say a Prayer

Dear God, help me to hear your will in sharing some of my time with the poorest of the poor.

Did you know? Pope John Paul II's father passed away at the age of sixty-two, on 18 February 1941.

My soul clings to you.

—Psalm 63:8

" The more you cling to Jesus the more capable you will become of being close to one another."

—Pope John Paul II, World Youth Day XII

Think About That

"Cling to Jesus." Now that's an interesting description of what we ought to do. Shut your eyes for a moment and let an image of "clinging to Jesus" come to you. What feelings does that image produce in you? Does it feel good to cling to Jesus?

Take Action

Every night this week, before you go to bed, spend fifteen minutes in quiet prayer. Let the image of clinging to Jesus enter your mind. If you have a Bible, read Hebrews 4:14, which tells us to cling to Jesus and to never stop trusting him.

Say a Prayer

Jesus, thank you for letting me cling to you. I pray that I will always trust you and that you will always be at my side.

Did you know? Pope John Paul II's birth name is Karol Wojtyla (pronounced Voy-tee-wah). He was born and raised near Krakow, Poland, under Nazism and the communist regime.

Do what is just and right.

—Ezekiel 45:9

❝ It is especially for you, young people, to take on the great task of *building a society where there will be more justice and solidarity.*❞

—Pope John Paul II, World Youth Day VI

Think About That

To build up a society in which we have more justice and solidarity, we must break down the barriers of hate and indifference. Hate is the opposite of justice, and indifference. Not caring prevents us from building solidarity. The Christian life leaves no room for hate or indifferences. We must love and we must care.

Take Action

In your school there is someone who experiences hatred or indifference from others. Who is that person or that group of people? What is one thing you will do this week to demonstrate care for that person or group of people?

Say a Prayer

Lord, help me to not have hate or indifference in my heart. Help me always to care about others and to treat others with love.

Did you know? John Paul II has traveled around the world more than any other pope in history. He has visited more than seventy countries since 1978.

The truth will make you free.

—John 8:32

cree

48

" Freedom is not the ability to do anything we want, whenever we want. Rather, freedom is the ability to live responsibly the truth of our relationship with God and one another."

—Pope John Paul II, Saint Louis, Missouri

Think About That

That's not what society would have us believe. The messages we get from society tell us that freedom is our opportunity to do whatever we want, no matter what. Well, that's not what freedom means for Christians. For us, freedom is something that comes from being in relationship with God. In that relationship we are freed to live a life of truth and a life that contributes to helping others.

Take Action

Set yourself free today. Do a kind act for someone at home, at school, or at work. After doing that kind act, pay attention to how you feel. That feeling is true freedom.

Say a Prayer

Lord, help me to do something kind for someone else today. In that act, help me to know what freedom really means. Thank you for the gift of freedom you have given me.

Did you know? In 1942, Pope John Paul II started working in a chemical plant in Solvay, Poland. Before that, he was a stonecutter.

Set the believers an example in speech and
conduct.

—1 Timothy 4:12

" Through her example, may [Most
Holy Mary] encourage you to be in
the new millennium announcers of
hope, love and peace."

—Pope John Paul II, World Youth Day XV

Think About That

Mary holds a special place in the church
because she was a great announcer of hope,
love, and peace. She said yes to God when she

was asked to be the mother of Jesus. Mary is also a great example to us in how we should live our life.

Take Action

This week, all week, you are asked to say yes to God. What is one thing you are going to say yes to that will please God and will bring about hope, love, or peace?

Say a Prayer

God, you are the source of hope, love, and peace. Grant me the strength to say yes to you this week, to be an instrument of your peace.

Did you know? Pope John Paul II was ordained a deacon on 20 October 1946.

Do not love the world.

—1 John 2:15

66 Let no one mislead you or prevent
you from seeing what really matters.
Turn to Jesus, listen to him, and
discover the true meaning and
direction of your lives."

—Pope John Paul II, Saint Louis, Missouri

Think About That

Think about all the advertisements you see in
one week on television or in magazines. They
are all trying to sell you something by telling
you that if you have what they are selling, you
will be happy. The Holy Father reminds us not
to be fooled. Only in Jesus will we find what
really matters and what really brings happiness.

Take Action

This week, find an old magazine that you can write in. Look at several of the advertisements. What are they telling you about "what really matters"? Do you believe it? If everyone in your family is finished reading the magazine write in your own positive, Christ-centered messages on the advertisements.

Say a Prayer

Lord, help me to know that you alone are what really matters. Help me to not be taken in by the many voices telling me that material things will bring me real happiness. Help me to trust in you.

Did you know? On 13 May 1981, at 5:19 p.m., while Pope John Paul II was circling in the popemobile in Saint Peter's Square, he was shot and severely wounded by a young Turkish man.

Let your light shine.

—Matthew 5:16

Care

66 You are ready for what Christ wants of you now. He wants you—all of you—to be the light of the world, as only young people can be light. It is time to let your light shine!"

—Pope John Paul II, Saint Louis, Missouri

Think About That

Interesting. The Holy Father says that you are ready for what Christ wants of you *now! Now* is the time for you to follow Christ. *Now* is the time for you to be the light of the world. *Now* is the time to let your light shine! He asks you not to wait until you are older, because you will never be more ready than you are right *now!*

Take Action

Quit waiting for the perfect moment. That time will never come. Instead, put down this book right *now* and go do a good deed. . . . Why are you still reading this page? Go do God's work right *now!* Do God's work all week.

Say a Prayer

Lord, now that I've realized that *now* is the time to do your will in the world, help me to never again say, "I'll do it when I'm older."

Did you know? In 1942, Pope John Paul II began studies for the priesthood in Krakow's secret seminary.

You will be my witnesses.

—Acts of the Apostles 1:8

" Dear young people, proclaiming the
Word of God is not the responsibility
of priests or religious alone, but it
is yours too. You must have the
courage to speak about Christ in
your families and in places where
you study, work or recreate. . . .
There are places and circumstances
where you alone can bring the seed
of God's Word."

—Pope John Paul II, World Youth Day VII

Think About That

Where are the places that "you alone" can share God's word with others? Do you know people through school, work, sports, or other activities that you can reach?

Take Action

Identify one person that you can share God's word with at school, at home, at work, or in some other place. Take time this week to talk with this person and to share God's word with them. You may share something you read in the Bible, or you may want to simply say kind words to them.

Say a Prayer

Lord, grant me the courage to accept the unique role I have in sharing your word with others.

Did you know? John Paul II was installed as the archbishop of Krakow, Poland, on 8 March 1964.

He would withdraw to deserted places and pray.

—Luke 5:16

" In prayer you become one with the
source of our true light, Jesus himself."

—Pope John Paul II, Saint Louis, Missouri

Think About That

We read throughout the Gospel stories in the
Bible that Jesus often went off to pray. Why? It
is in prayer that we are alone with God, in
conversation with God. In prayer we can quiet
ourselves enough to listen to God, and in
listening and believing, we become one with
God.

Take Action

Every night this week, take 20 minutes before you go to bed to spend time in prayer. First, quiet yourself. Then, open your Bible to any page and let your eyes fall on a section. Read that section slowly. Now, be quiet; reflect on what you read and listen to what you hear in your heart. Stay quiet and listen for at least 10 minutes.

Say a Prayer

Jesus, be with me when I pray to your Father as you did. Help me to be still and to listen to what God has to say to me today.

Did you know? In 1956, Pope John Paul II was appointed chair of ethics at the Catholic University of Lublin.

Consider your own call.

—1 Corinthians 1:26

" I hope that many young men and women, inspired by sincere, apostolic zeal, will consecrate their own lives to Christ and the Church as priests and religious, or as lay people who are also ready to leave their own countries to rush to those places where workers in Christ's vineyard are scarce."

—Pope John Paul II, World Youth Day VII

Think About That

What is Christ calling you to do? If called, would you be willing to give your life to serve Christ as a priest, a nun, or a brother? Perhaps

you are being called to work as a lay missionary. Would you be willing to give your life to
serve as a missionary, going to places where
few would be willing to go?

Take Action

This week, find an adult whom you respect and
trust and schedule a 30-minute meeting with
him or her. When you meet, ask if he or she
could see you serving Christ as a priest, a
vowed religious, or a missionary someday. Ask
what talents or gifts that person sees in you that
could be used to serve others.

Say a Prayer

Dear Lord, help me to be open to your calling.
Lead me to others who can help me figure out
how I am called to serve you.

Did you know? The pope had just one brother, Edmund, who was a
physician.

Commit your work to the Lord.

—Proverbs 16:3

" Remember: Christ is calling you; the Church needs you; the Pope believes in you and he expects great things of you!"

—Pope John Paul II, Saint Louis, Missouri

Think About That

The Holy Father has great confidence in you, in your spirit and energy and talents. He believes that you can do great things right now. He believes that you can show the world that peace is possible. He believes that you can bring joy to others through kindness, mercy, charity, and forgiveness. Not only does he believe you can do it, he *expects* it of you!

Take Action

This week, you are going to do something great for others. What will it be? Choose one thing you can actually do that you think the pope would consider to be a "great thing." Now, when are you going to do it? How are you going to do it?

Say a Prayer

Lord, guide me in figuring out what "great thing" I can do this week. Give me the courage to not just think about it but to do it!

Did you know? In 1940, Pope John Paul II was able to evade deportation and imprisonment by the Nazis by working as a stonecutter in a quarry at Krakow.

You need endurance.

—Hebrews 10:36

" Be in this world bearers of Christian faith and hope by living love every day. Be faithful witnesses of the Risen Christ, never turn back before the obstacles that present themselves on the paths of your lives.

I am counting on you. On your youthful energy and your dedication to Christ."

—Pope John Paul II, Poznan, Poland

Think About That

The Holy Father was a young person once, and knows well how obstacles can get in the way of our being witnesses of Christian faith. He also knows how big an impact youthful energy can have in making a difference in the world. He knows that when youthful energy is dedicated to Christ, it can change the world.

Take Action

Find a small stone that will fit easily in your pocket. This stone represents your dedication to Christ when you encounter obstacles each day. Carry this stone in your pocket all week long. Each time you encounter an obstacle, reach in your pocket and feel the stone. Remember that it is your dedication to Christ that will allow you to overcome the obstacle.

Say a Prayer

Lord, you alone can help me move past the obstacles I run into. Help me to always trust in your presence.

Did you know? Pope John Paul II is the first non-Italian pontiff since the sixteenth century.

Honor your father and your mother.

—Exodus 20:12

66 I am thinking especially of your
parents, who cooperate with God in
giving you life and in caring for you:
honor them and be grateful for
them!"

—Pope John Paul II, World Youth Day XIV

Think About That

Have you ever stopped to think about how
your parental figures are "cooperators" with
God? They work with God by loving us and

working to provide for our needs. Their love for us comes from God. Sometimes we fail to recognize that.

Take Action

One night this week, make dinner for your parents. Have a cake with candles to celebrate your gratitude for them. Use party favors—hats, noisemakers, and balloons—to make the dinner a real celebration.

Say a Prayer

Lord, I don't always show it, but I am so grateful for my parents, for all they do for me. They love me because you love them. Thank you for that.

Did you know? Pope John Paul II has made five pastoral visits to the United States.

Do not lag in zeal.

—Romans 12:11

" I am told that there was much excitement in Saint Louis during the recent baseball season, when two great players (Mark McGwire and Sammy Sosa) were competing to break the home run record. You can feel the same great enthusiasm as you train for a different goal: the goal of following Christ, the goal of bringing his message to the world."

—Pope John Paul II, Saint Louis, Missouri

Think About That

Think about how much time we spend preparing for our sporting teams, musical programs, or other activities we enjoy. What would happen if we spent just as much time preparing to follow Christ and to bring Christ's message to the world?

Take Action

This week, devote all your energy to a spiritual training session. Write out a training plan. What will you do in the mornings, the afternoons, and the evenings to practice following Christ? At the end of the week, look back over your training plan, and ask yourself how well you did.

Say a Prayer

Lord, help me to dedicate myself to you with the same amount of energy I spend practicing sports, music, or other activities I enjoy.

Did you know? On 13 April 1929, Pope John Paul II's mother passed away at the age of forty-five.

Forgive, and you will be forgiven.

—Luke 6:37

" In this Sacrament [Reconciliation]
. . . you are freed from sin and
from its ugly companion which is
shame. Your burdens are lifted and
you experience the joy of new life in
Christ."

—Pope John Paul II, Saint Louis, Missouri

Think About That

Shame is that bad feeling we have when we
know we have done something wrong—
something that goes against what God wants us
to do. The way to get rid of the burden of

shame is to seek forgiveness and to live our life like Jesus did from now on. When we do that, joy is the feeling we have inside.

Take Action

When is the last time you received the sacrament of Reconciliation? Check with your parish to see when the sacrament is offered this week. Plan on receiving the sacrament to experience the lifting of the burden of shame that the Holy Father speaks of.

Say a Prayer

Lord, help me to know that when I feel shame, it is because I have done something that goes against your will. Help me to forgive others and to ask for forgiveness from others when I do something wrong. Fill me with the feeling of joy.

Did you know? Pope John Paul II was nearly killed by an assassin in 1981. Instead of harboring a lot of hatred toward his would-be killer, Pope John Paul II went to the prison where the assassin was being held and forgave him.

We have gifts that differ.

—Romans 12:6

" Little by little you recognize the 'talent' or 'talents' which each of you has, and you begin to use them in a creative way, you begin to increase them."

—Pope John Paul II, *Dilecti Amici*

Think About That

Talents are funny things. The more you recognize them, the more you use them, and the more you use them, the more you develop them. Talents grow, but only if we use them.

Take Action

What is one talent that you have? This week, find three creative ways to use that talent. At the end of the week, ask yourself, "What did I learn about myself by using this talent?"

Say a Prayer

Lord, my talents are gifts from you. Thank you for these gifts. Help me to use my talents for the good of others so that my talents will grow to accomplish your will.

Did you know? The pope is also a civil ruler, serving as the head of state of the Vatican City, which has a population of about a thousand people.

I will sing to the Lord as long as I live.

—Psalm 104:33

66 It is first of all necessary for you
young people to give a forceful
witness of love for life, God's gift.
This love must extend from the
beginning to the end of every life."

—Pope John Paul II, World Youth Day XI

Think About That

Life is a gift from God. Anything that takes away
life or diminishes life denies God's gift. This is
the opposite of love, and the opposite of love is

sin. The taking of human life before it is born is a denial of God's love. Taking a human life in any form at any time is contrary to God's love. We always must promote and protect life.

Take Action

This week, ask your mom or dad to tell you about the time when you were born or adopted. Ask them to describe how they felt when you were born or adopted, how they felt about the gift you were to them.

Say a Prayer

Lord, help me to always promote and protect life, the life of the unborn, the life of the vulnerable, the life of the elderly.

Did you know? In 1985, Pope John Paul II started the first International Youth Meeting, which has become the annual World Youth Day.

May he so strengthen your hearts in holiness.

—1 Thessalonians 3:13

"Do not be afraid to be holy! Have the courage and humility to present yourselves to the world determined to be holy, since full, true freedom is born from holiness."

—Pope John Paul II, Santiago, Spain

Think About That

Sometimes we are afraid to be holy because we think it means that we have to be better than others. But holiness isn't about being better than others. It is about living our life like Jesus lived his life. It is that simple.

Take Action

Write down three ways in which you are a holy person. In other words, write down three ways in which you already live your life like Jesus lived his life. Now, write down three more ways in which you'd like to live your life more like Jesus. This week, your goal is to try to live like Jesus, especially in these three additional ways.

Say a Prayer

Jesus, help me to not be afraid to live my life in the way you lived your life. Help me to be more like you each day.

Did you know? John Paul II has received many of the world's important political leaders during his papacy.

Set free from sin . . .

—Romans 6:18

" To be truly free does not at all mean
doing everything that pleases me, or
doing what I want to do. . . . To be
truly free means to use one's own
freedom for what is a true good."

—Pope John Paul II, *Dilecti Amici*

Think About That

As we grow up, especially in our teenage years,
we begin to learn more about what freedom
means. We get to do things that we never could

before. The trap is that we can begin to think that we can do whatever we want to do. But if we call ourselves Christians then we must always do what Jesus would do.

Take Action

Make ten small cards with this phrase written on them: "Set yourself free. Do something good for someone else today!" Distribute the cards to ten people you know, and ask them to take action on the saying within one week. Tell them it's like their "get-out-of-jail free" card from Monopoly.

Say a Prayer

Lord, help me to feel truly free by doing what you ask of me, rather than by doing whatever I feel like doing, regardless of what it is.

Did you know? The large, pointed hat worn by the pope is called a mitre. It is a ceremonial headdress worn for liturgical celebrations.

A lamp shining in a dark place . . .

—2 Peter 1:19

" Remember what Jesus said: 'I am the light of the world; those who follow me will not walk in darkness, but will have the light of life' [John 8:12, NAB]."

—Pope John Paul II, Saint Louis, Missouri

Think About That

The light of the world is Jesus. Jesus' life is the light of the world. The popular phrase, "What Would Jesus Do?" is another way of saying, "What is the light that Jesus sheds in the world?" When we have light, we can see things as they really are. But in darkness we can't see clearly. We need light to see what's real, what's true. Jesus is the light! Jesus is real! Jesus is the truth!

80

Take Action

Turn off the lights in your room so you have complete darkness. Now, close your eyes and walk around the room. Notice that you are more cautious than you would be if the lights were on and your eyes were open. This week, think about this experience when you see an opportunity to do what Jesus would do. In other words, reveal the light of life, the light of Jesus Christ, when you see others stumbling in the dark.

Say a Prayer

Jesus, you are the light of my life. Help me to always see the world through your eyes so that I may be more like you every day.

Did you know? Pope John Paul II celebrated his first Mass at the crypt of Saint Leonard at Wawel, on 2 November 1946.

The ways of life . . .

—Acts of the Apostles 2:28

" It is along the paths of daily life that you can meet the Lord!"

—Pope John Paul II, World Youth Day XII

Think About That

When you wake up each morning, think about the "path" you take through your house to get ready for the day. Now, where along that path might you "meet the Lord"? Is the Lord in your brother or sister as they rush for the same bathroom? Is the Lord is in your mom or dad as they get breakfast ready for you?

Take Action

This week, as you walk along the paths to wherever you are going, keep your eyes open for the Lord. At the end of each day, name one place where you saw the Lord along the paths of your life.

Say a Prayer

Lord, I know that you are everywhere. You are in the people I meet every day. Please, help me today to see you in the faces of my family, my friends, my teachers, and even strangers.

Did you know? The pope's paternal grandparents were Maciej and Anna Wojtyla. His paternal grandfather was a master tailor.

Draw near to God.

—James 4:8

" Dear young people, like the first disciples, *follow Jesus!* Do not be afraid to draw near to Him, to cross the threshold of His dwelling, to speak to Him face to face, as you talk with a friend."

—Pope John Paul II, World Youth Day XII

Think About That

Take a minute to think about the best conversation you have ever had with a friend. What did you talk about? How did it feel to talk openly and honestly with a friend? That's how we are to talk with Jesus—as if he is our best friend, someone we can tell anything to, with whom our secrets are safe.

Take Action

This week, write a letter to Jesus as if he were your best friend. What do you want to tell him? What do you want him to know about you? What do you want to ask him? What do you want to know about him?

Say a Prayer

Jesus, thank you for being my friend. I am happy to know that I can talk to you as I would talk to my best friend.

Did you know? The pope's maternal grandparents were Feliks and Anna Kaczorowska. His maternal grandfather was a packsaddle maker.

Testify to the light.

—John 1:8

" Do not be afraid of presenting Christ to someone who does not yet know Him."

—Pope John Paul II, World Youth Day VII

Think About That

This is a big challenge that the Holy Father presents to us. We meet people each day that do not yet know about Christ. We are asked to present Christ to them both in the way we live and in the way we treat them. We also must tell them about Christ and his good work.

Take Action

Do you know someone who does not yet know Christ—someone who is not a Christian? This week, take time to talk with that person. Invite him or her to come to Mass with you sometime or to join you at a youth group meeting or some other activity as a way to get to know about Christ and the church.

Say a Prayer

Lord, your word is so wonderful, such good news, that I want to share it with others, especially those who have not yet had a chance to get to know you. Give me the courage to share your word with them.

Did you know? Pope John Paul II was consecrated cardinal at the Sistine Chapel on 28 June 1967.

"Keep up your courage!"

—Acts of the Apostles 23:11

" As disciples and friends of Jesus, become agents of dialogue and collaboration with those who believe in God who rules the universe with infinite love."

—Pope John Paul II, World Youth Day XII

Think About That

What exactly is the Holy Father asking us to do? He's asking you to talk about your faith in God and to work together with others who believe in God. Why? So that God's love can reach all people. There is no limit to the good things that can come from sharing God's love with our friends and our community. He is asking you to be a friend of Jesus both in what you say and how you live your life.

Take Action

In your group of friends, who do you know that also believes in God? Today, get the courage to talk to that friend about God. Ask what she or he believes about God and why believing in God is important to her or him.

Say a Prayer

God, grant me the courage to talk about you with my friends. I know that good things will come from this conversation.

Did you know? Pope John Paul II was voted *Time* magazine's "Man of the Year" in 1994 because of his determination to promote moral values throughout the world.

Be at peace among yourselves.

—1 Thessalonians, 5:13

" None of us is alone in this world; each of us is a vital piece of the great mosaic of humanity as a whole."

—Pope John Paul II, Israel-Palestine

Think About That

In speaking to the young people in Israel and Palestine, John Paul II is addressing people who have been at war with one another for more than two thousand years. The Holy Father believes that young people can be peacemakers. In fact, he believes that young people have a unique opportunity to be builders of peace in this world. We can change the way the history unfolds by recognizing that we all need one another. We must live in peace.

Take Action

This week, when you find yourself in an argument with someone else, stop and ask yourself, "What can I do in this situation to make peace between us?" Ask the person you are arguing with this simple question, "What can we do to make peace?" At Mass on Sunday, during the sign of peace, remember this situation and feel in your heart what real peace means.

Say a Prayer

Lord, help me to be a peacemaker among my friends.

Did you know? If you were to total the miles the Holy Father has traveled outside of Rome, it would be equivalent to traveling more than 27 times the earth's circumference, or more than 2.7 times the distance between the earth and the moon.

Faith is the assurance of things hoped for.

—Hebrews 11:1

" Christ freed Peter from the fear which had seized him on the stormy lake. Christ enables us too to overcome the difficult moments in life, if with faith and hope we turn to him and ask his help."

—Pope John Paul II, Poznan, Poland

Think About That

Faith and hope are the opposites of fear. Fear will always paralyze us and keep us from doing what we could do if we were not fearful. In the difficult moments of life it is easy to give in to our fear, but it is in these moments that we must have the greatest trust in the Lord.

Take Action

This week, you will experience something difficult. When it happens, pause and say a prayer. Ask God to help you. Ask God to give you faith and hope so that you can make it through the difficult experience.

Say a Prayer

Dear God, when life is difficult, help me to turn to you rather than to be consumed by fear and doubt. I know that in you all things are possible and that you love me.

Did you know? The pope earned his doctorate degree in theology from the Angelicum University in Rome.

It is easier for a camel to go through the eye of a
needle.

—Matthew 19:24

66 The human person, created in the
image and likeness of God, cannot
become a slave to things, to eco-
nomic systems, to technological
civilization, to consumerism, to easy
success."

—Pope John Paul II, Poznan, Poland

Think About That

Because we are created in the image of God,
our whole life is meant to be about loving our
neighbors and loving God. When we get caught
up in all the stuff of life, like money, computer
games, buying cool clothes, or finding the easy
way out, we are distracted from what really
matters—caring for and about others.

Take Action

How much time in a given week do you spend on each of the following activities?

- earning money
- buying things
- playing or chatting on the computer
- playing video games
- finding ways to make your life easier
- praying
- doing good deeds for others

How do you spend most of your time? How do you want to spend most of your time? What does God ask of you? This week, find some answers to this questions.

Say a Prayer

Lord, help me to spend my time on the things that matter in life, rather than on all the distractions that are available to me.

Did you know? The pope's father was also named Karol Wojtyla, and he was born on 18 July 1879.

Teach me to do your will.

—Psalm 143:10

" I want to invite you this year to fix

your eyes on Jesus, Teacher and

Lord of life."

—Pope John Paul II, World Youth Day XII

Think About That

We tend to "fix our eyes" on things that we find attractive, right? Well, fixing our eyes on Jesus means that we find him and his ways attractive to us. By fixing our eyes on him, we can learn more about him, as we study his ways and his life.

Take Action

Do you have a crucifix or a cross in your room?
If not, perhaps you might get one to hang on
a wall. You also may have some other sacred
object or a copy of the sacred Scriptures. Fix
your eyes on this object or on the Scriptures.
See Jesus before you. Ask, "What can I learn
from Jesus, the teacher, today?"

Say a Prayer

Lord, help me to fix my eyes on you each day,
to find you attractive so that I might live like
you. Teach me your ways.

Did you know? In 1940, Pope John Paul II met a spiritual friend, Jan
Tryanowski, who introduced him to the spiritual writings of John of the
Cross and Teresa of Ávila.

I am the way, and the truth, and the life.

—John 14:6

" Talk with Jesus in prayer while listening to the Word; experience the joy of reconciliation in the sacrament of Penance; receive the Body and Blood of Christ in the Eucharist; welcome and serve Him in your brothers and sisters."

—Pope John Paul II, World Youth Day XII

Think About That

The Holy Father is describing for us the way to be disciples of Jesus. First, read the Bible and listen to God's word. Second, forgive others and be forgiven through the sacrament of Penance.

Third, attend Mass and receive Christ in the Eucharist. After doing these things—hearing the word, receiving forgiveness, and taking the Eucharist—go forth and serve others as Christ did.

Take Action

This week, practice each of the four steps mentioned above. Read from your Bible at least once this week. Seek forgiveness from someone, and receive the sacrament of Penance if possible. Attend Mass. Commit to one thing that is of service to others, such as volunteering or helping out at your school or in the community.

Say a Prayer

Lord, I want to follow your ways. Help me to hear your word, forgive others, receive you in the Eucharist, and serve those in need.

Did you know? Pope John Paul II participated in the sessions of the Second Vatican Council beginning in October 1962 and ending in 1965.

To you I lift up my eyes.

—Psalm 123:1

" Dear young people, . . . learn to

lift your hearts in an attitude of

contemplation."

—Pope John Paul II, World Youth Day XV

Think About That

Contemplation is about being present to something. When you are present to someone, you
are completely there for him or her, paying full
attention. That's what we are asked to do each
day with Jesus. We are asked to be completely
present, to pay full attention to and listen to
Jesus in our heart every day.

Take Action

Contemplation is something we can learn, but it takes practice. So today, practice contemplation. When you get in a situation that requires you to make a choice about something, pause before deciding, and contemplate what Jesus would do or say. Try this each time you are faced with a choice, and soon you will be doing it naturally.

Say a Prayer

Lord, help me learn how to be present to you in all the situations of my life. Thank you for being present to me always.

Did you know? In 1944, the Russians freed Krakow from Nazi occupation. In that same year, Pope John Paul II entered his third year of theological studies, in preparation for the priesthood.

Do nothing from selfish ambition or conceit.

—Philippians 2:3

" Selfishness makes people deaf and

dumb; love opens eyes and hearts."

—Pope John Paul II, World Youth Day XI

Think About That

Selfishness is caring only about yourself. When
you are so consumed with caring only about
yourself, you can't hear the needs of others and
you can't speak words of concern for others.
Instead of being selfish, Jesus calls us to love.
Love is the opposite of selfishness; it opens us
up to others, and it causes us to want to give of
ourselves to others.

Take Action

We all have moments when we are selfish. Identify one thing you do that is an act of selfishness. How can you convert your selfishness to an act of love?

Say a Prayer

Lord, you know when I am selfish. Help me to recognize when I am acting selfishly and to choose instead to act with love and concern for others.

Did you know? On 16 October 1978, Pope John Paul II was elected the 264th pope at approximately 5:15 p.m.

The road is hard that leads to life.

—Matthew 7:14

Cite

" The way Jesus shows you is not easy. Rather, it is like a path winding up a mountain. Do not lose heart! The steeper the road, the faster it raises towards ever-wider horizons."

—Pope John Paul II, World Youth Day XI

Think About That

The Holy Father doesn't pretend that following Jesus is going to be easy. Jesus himself didn't hide that fact either. Remember the rich young man who met Jesus in Matthew, chapter 19? He wanted eternal life, but when Jesus told him it wouldn't be easy, he went away. Don't go away. Stay the course, because it leads to great things.

Take Action

What is the hardest thing that you think Jesus asks of you? Write it down on a piece of paper. Now, write out a prayer to Jesus that asks him to help follow him even when the road gets steep. Place the piece of paper in your dresser drawer. Each time this week that you feel it is too hard to follow Jesus, pull out that piece of paper and say the prayer.

Say a Prayer

Jesus, even though it is difficult to follow you at times, be patient with me. I want to follow you even when it is not easy.

Did you know? In September 1987, while visiting San Francisco, Pope John Paul II met with AIDS patients and embraced a little boy named Brendan, as a sign of his compassion and affection for ill people.

If the Lord wishes . . .

—James 4:15

66 The Lord will help you to know his will; he will help you to follow your vocation courageously."

—Pope John Paul II, Saint Louis, Missouri

Think About That

God wills something wonderful for each of us. We each have a special vocation in life. Some of us will be called to be witnesses of Christ through marriage, some through single life, some through vowed religious life, and some through ordained priesthood. Each vocation requires courage to follow its path.

Take Action

This week, find people who have followed each of these four vocations (married life, single life, vowed religious life, ordained priesthood), and talk with each one about their life. Ask them about the courage it takes to follow their vocation. Ask them how the Lord helped them to know his will.

Say a Prayer

Lord, grant me the courage to follow whatever vocation I am called to in my life. Whatever my vocation might be, help me to always give witness to your will.

Did you know? In May 1938, Pope John Paul II received the sacrament of Confirmation.

Awesome is God.

—Psalm 68:35

" What must I do? 'What must I do to inherit eternal life?' What must I do so that my life may have full value and meaning? The youth of each one of you, dear friends, is a treasure that is manifested precisely in these questions."

—Pope John Paul II, *Dilecti Amici*

Think About That

Our youth is a time in which we ask a lot of important questions. For example, we ask: "Who will I be when I grow up? What will I do

with my life? What is the meaning of life?"
These are good questions, and it is Christ alone
who has the answers. We must always turn to
Christ for the answers.

Take Action

Take out a piece of paper and a pen. Write at
the top of the paper, "My Questions." Carry the
piece of paper with you all week. Each time
you have a question about life, write that
question down. At the end of the week, look
over the questions you have written down and
spend time in prayer with God, asking God to
help you find the answers.

Say a Prayer

Lord, you know me better than anyone does.
You know my questions. Help me to find the
answers.

Did you know? The pope lives in the Vatican Palace, which is in its
own city-state, called the Vatican City, in the middle of Rome.

There is no fear in love.

—1 John 4:18

" Break down the barriers of super-

ficiality and fear!"

—Pope John Paul II, World Youth Day XII

Think About That

Superficiality is when we won't open ourselves up for people to really know us. Fear is the inability to trust that things will be okay. Both of these ways of acting create barriers. They prevent others from getting to know us as we really are, and they prevent us from getting to know others for whom they really are. They even prevent us from completely knowing God.

Take Action

In what areas of life do you fear to trust others? Can you identify one way that your fear puts up barriers with others? This week, see if you can step beyond that fear to do that which your fear keeps you from doing.

Say a Prayer

Lord, help me to not be afraid, especially of sharing my true self with others and of accepting others as they are.

Did you know? In 1939, the year that the Second World War began, Pope John Paul II enrolled in his second year of university courses in literature and philosophy at Jagiellonian University.

. . . vanity of vanities!

—Ecclesiastes 1:2

66 Dear young people, you are under threat from the bad use of advertising techniques, which plays upon the natural tendency to avoid effort and promises the immediate satisfaction of every desire, while consumerism that goes with it suggests that [you] should seek self-fulfillment especially in the enjoyment of material goods."

—Pope John Paul II, *Dilecti Amici*

Think About That

The advertisements that you see every day are powerful, convincing, and pull with great strength to get you to believe that material things will make you happy. But you can have all the money in the world and still be lonely, sad, and empty inside. The message that a product can solve all your problems is a lie.

Take Action

Contact a retirement home in your community and ask if you can visit some of the residents. Talk to at least two residents about their life, and ask them from their perspective what really matters in life.

Say a Prayer

God, help me to focus my attention on those things that really matter in life.

Did you know? The pope's first pastoral visit outside of Italy was to the Dominican Republic, Mexico, and the Bahamas in January 1979.

Keep yourself pure.

—1 Timothy 5:22

" Do not listen to those who tell you that chastity is *passé.* In your hearts you know that true love is a gift from God and respects his plan for the union of man and woman in marriage."

—Pope John Paul II, Saint Louis, Missouri

Think About That

The church teaches that the union between the physical body and the spiritual life is sacred. So, the most intimate ways of expressing our sexuality are always to be tied to the gift of love in the context of marriage. But lots of voices will tell you otherwise. Don't be fooled by those voices.

Take Action

This week, pay attention to all the voices that tell you that premarital sex is just something that teens do. When you hear that voice, pause and remember that these are false truths. Choose to live a chaste life.

Say a Prayer

Lord, help me, when I'm surrounded by temptations, to live a chaste life. And help me to remember that, if it is your will, I might someday enjoy the fullness of your love in marriage.

Did you know? Pope John Paul II's older brother, Edmund, died on 5 December 1932, at the age of twenty-six.

Pray in the Spirit at all times in every prayer.

—Ephesians 6:18

" Pray and learn to pray! . . . Deepen your knowledge of the Word of the Living God by reading and meditating on the Scriptures."

—Pope John Paul II, *Dilecti Amici*

Think About That

We come to know God better through prayer and through reading and meditating on the Scriptures. Praying is more than just saying words. It is entering into a conversation with God. We can enter prayer by first reading from the Bible and then meditating on what we have read. From there we can talk to and listen to God.

Take Action

In your Bible, read the story of Jesus praying in Gethsemane (Mark 14:32–42). After reading the story, sit quietly. What are your thoughts after reading this story? Enter into a conversation with God about your thoughts.

Say a Prayer

Lord, teach me to pray as you did in Gethsemane. I want to be a faithful disciple that "stays awake" in our relationship.

Did you know? The pope was always a good student. He received high marks from elementary school through graduate studies.

Topic Index

Acknowledgments *(continued)*

Unless otherwise noted, the scriptural passages in this book are taken from *The Catholic Youth Bible,* New Revised Standard Version, Catholic Edition. Copyright © 2001 by Saint Mary's Press. All rights reserved.

The scriptural passage marked NAB, on page 80, is from the New American Bible with revised Psalms and revised New Testament. Copyright © 1991, 1986, and 1970 by the Confraternity of Christian Doctrine, 3211 Fourth Street NE, Washington, DC 20017. All rights reserved.

Selections from the Holy Father's speeches, homilies, addresses, and greetings are reprinted by permission of *L'Osservatore Romano.*

The statistic on page 91 is from *www.catholic-pages.com/pope/ johnpaul2.asp,* accessed 20 February 2001.

About the Author

John M. Vitek serves as the president of Saint Mary's Press. Over the past nineteen years, he has served the church as a diocesan chancellor and as a director of a variety of pastoral programs. John is on the faculty of the graduate program in pastoral ministries at Saint Mary's University in Winona, Minnesota. He is the author of *A Companion Way,* published by Saint Mary's Press. John resides on a farm outside of Winona with his wife and four children, where they raise llamas.